P9-AQX-938

cloverleaf books™

Fall's Here!

Animals in Fall

Preparing for Winter

Martha E. H. Rustad

illustrated by Amanda Enright

MILLBROOK PRESS · MINNEAPOLIS

For my husband—M.E.H.R.

Millbrook Press
A division of Lerner Publishing Group, Inc.
241 First Avenue North
Minneapolis, MN 55401 U.S.A.

Website address: www.lernerbooks.com

Main body text set in Slappy Inline 18/28.
Typeface provided by T26.

Library of Congress Cataloging-in-Publication Data

Rustad, Martha E. H. (Martha Elizabeth Hillman), 1975–
Animals in fall : preparing for winter / by Martha E. H. Rustad ; illustrated by Amanda Enright.
p. cm. — (Cloverleaf books--fall's here!)
Includes index.
ISBN 978-0-7613-5066-8 (lib. bdg. : alk. paper)
1. Animal behavior—Juvenile literature. 2. Autumn—Juvenile literature. 3. Winter—Juvenile literature. I. Enright, Amanda, ill. II. Title.
QL751.5.R875 2012
578.4'3—dc22
2010053468

Manufactured in the United States of America
2 - BP - 8/1/12

TABLE OF CONTENTS

Chapter One
Animals in Fall

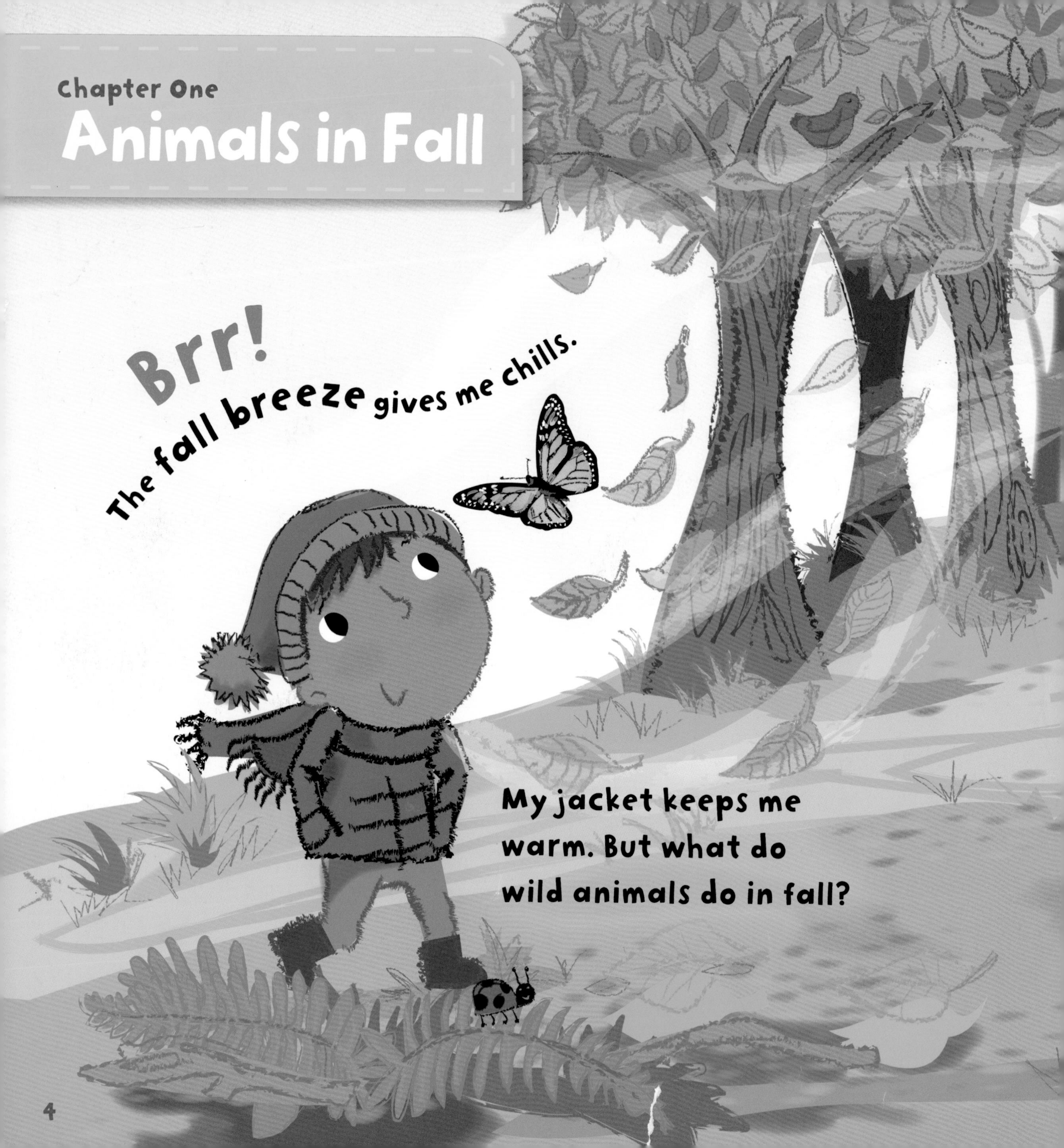

Brr!

The fall breeze gives me chills.

My jacket keeps me warm. But what do wild animals do in fall?

Animals know cool weather and shorter days mean summer is over. In fall, animals get **ready for winter.** Some animals go south. Some go to sleep. And some change.

Animals that go south in the fall migrate. Animals that sleep for the winter hibernate.

Chapter Two

Some Animals Go South

Whoosh! Gray whales spout through their blowholes.

Gray whales have their babies near Mexico. The waters there are safe and warm.

All summer, they eat to build up a fat called blubber. In fall, gray whales swim from Alaska to Mexico. They live off the blubber as they migrate.

Flutter!

Monarch butterflies fly south in fall.

They usually fly all morning.

They eat in the afternoon.

They rest all night.
They cannot live in cold weather. They migrate as far as 3,000 miles (4,800 kilometers).

Millions of monarch butterflies rest together in trees. The branches of the trees sometimes bend down from the weight of so many butterflies.

Honk! Canada geese fly low across the sky. They form a V-shape.

When northern lakes freeze, Canada geese migrate south. They stop to eat and rest on open water along the way.

A flock of Canada geese often flies the same route each year. It also stops to rest in the same places.

Chapter Three
Some Animals Sleep

Grr! Black bears gobble fruits and nuts in the fall. They gain as much as 30 pounds (14 kilograms) each week.

Black bears look for a small den.
They sleep in this safe place
when cold weather comes.

Black bears hibernate for most of winter. But sometimes, they wake up on very warm days. They might go look for food. Then they go back to sleep.

Ssss! Rattlesnakes slither to their dens in fall.

They hibernate in caves or holes in the ground that will not freeze.

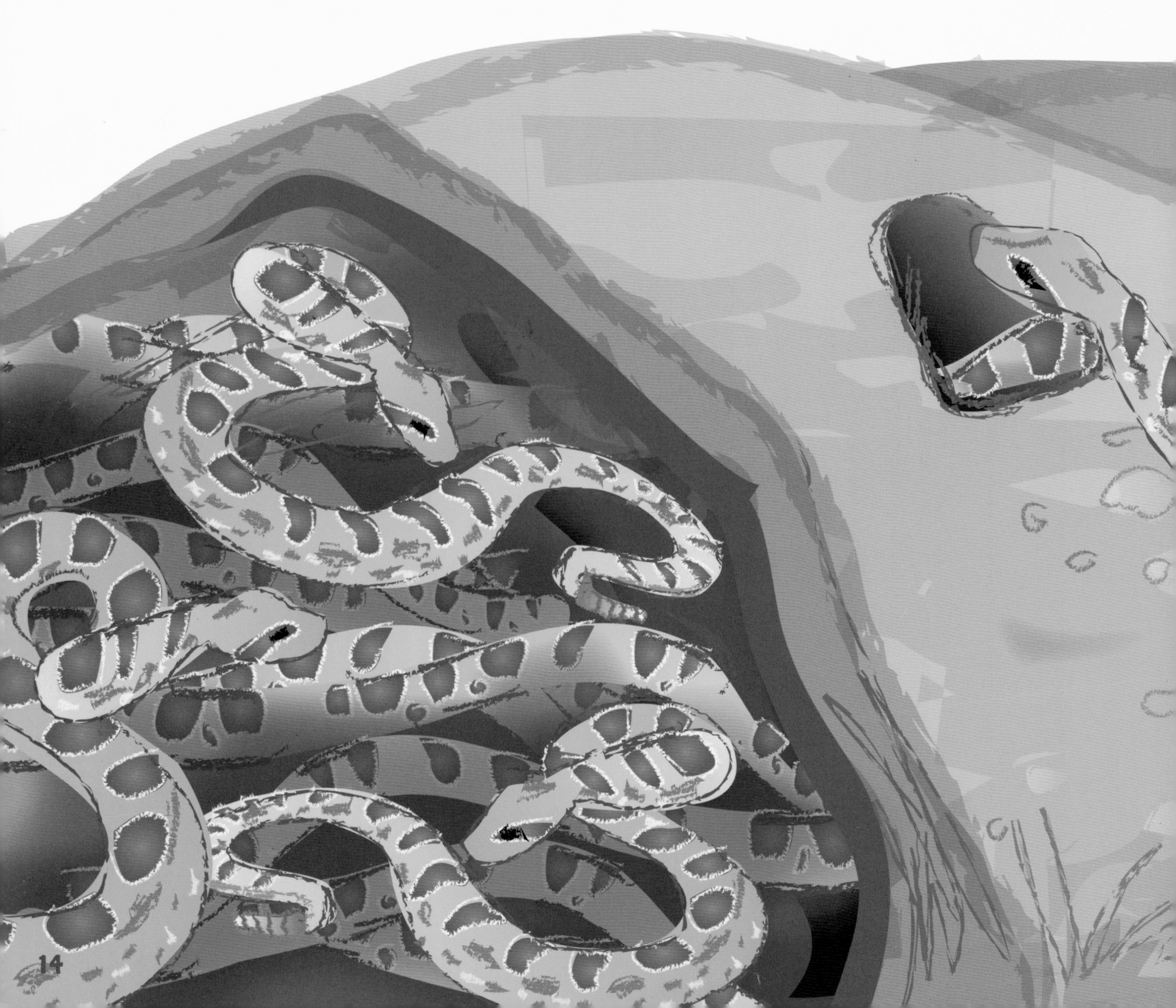

Hundreds of snakes may gather in one place. Rattlesnakes often return to the same den each year.

Young rattlesnakes are born in fall. They sometimes do not eat until spring.

Chapter Four

Some Animals Change

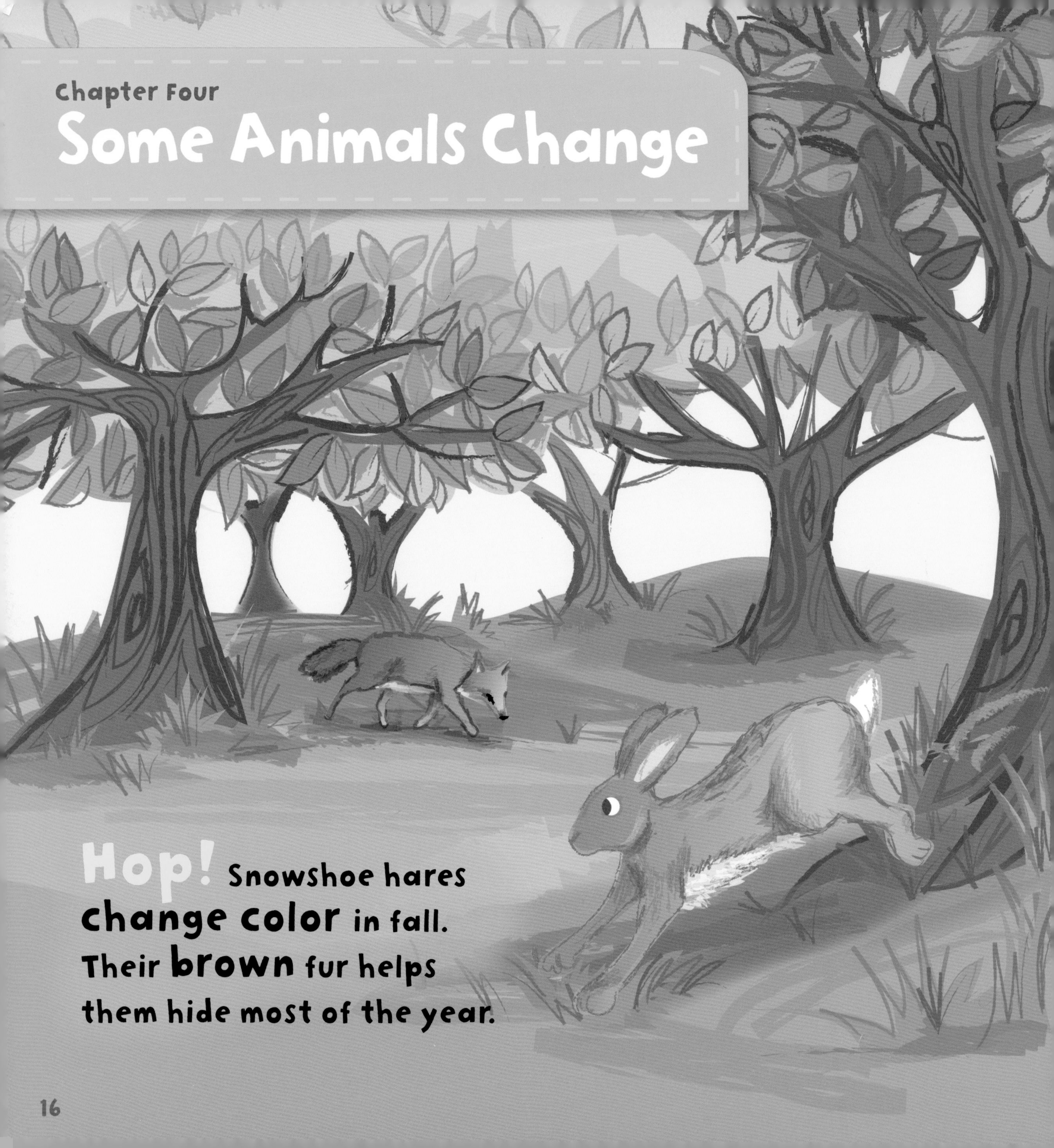

Hop! Snowshoe hares **change color** in fall. Their **brown** fur helps them hide most of the year.

But in winter, they must be **white** to match the snow.

This color **protects** them from animals that might eat them.

Munch! White-tailed deer crunch acorns and grind leaves in fall.

Eating lots of food helps deer get extra fat on their bodies. They live off their fat during the winter. Food is harder to find in winter.

White-tailed deer grow thicker coats in the fall. Their coats keep them warm.

Chapter Five
Ready for Winter

Look! I see the first snowflakes.

Fall is over.

Winter is here.

The animals are ready.

Blubber Gloves Activity

In fall, many animals eat extra food. The extra food gives their bodies more fat. Some animals live off their extra fat during winter. Ocean animals have a layer of fat called blubber. It keeps the animals warm. In this activity, you will get to feel what it is like to have blubber.

Equipment:

bucket
cold tap water
ice
rubber gloves (surgical or cleaning)
rubber spatula
vegetable shortening (such as Crisco)
quart-size zippered bags

Steps:

1) Fill a bucket halfway full of cold tap water. Put your hand in the water. How does it feel?

2) Add ice to the bucket, but don't fill it to the top. Put your hand in the water. Does it feel different?

3) Put on a rubber glove. Put your hand in the water. Does it feel the same or different from in step 2?

4) Using the rubber spatula, spread vegetable shortening on your gloved hand. Be sure to coat your hand evenly. Put your hand in the bag, and zip it shut as far as you can. Put your hand in the water. How does the water feel now? Does the extra fat keep your hand warmer?

GLOSSARY

blowholes: holes on the tops of ocean mammals' heads for breathing

blubber: a layer of fat in ocean animals

coats: the fur on animals

den: a home for a wild animal, such as a bear or a rattlesnake

fat: a material in bodies that gives animals energy and keeps them warm

flutter: to lightly flap

gather: to come together

gobble: to eat food quickly

hibernate: to spend the winter in a deep sleep. Hibernating animals have slower heart rates, slower breathing rates, and lower body temperatures. Animals sometimes wake up to eat and pass waste.

migrate: to move from one area to another in fall or spring

munch: to chew

open water: ponds, lakes, rivers, and other places with water that is not frozen

route: a way, path, or road animals follow to get from one place to another

slither: to move like a snake

spout: to push or shoot something out with force

TO LEARN MORE

BOOKS

Andersen, Sheila. *Are You Ready for Fall?* Minneapolis: Lerner Publications Company, 2010. This book uses photos to explore the things we see and experience in fall.

Frost, Helen. *Monarch and Milkweed.* New York: Atheneum Books for Young Readers, 2008. Read about the life cycles of monarch butterflies and milkweed plants.

Glaser, Linda. *Not a Buzz to Be Found: Insects in Winter.* Minneapolis: Millbrook Press, 2012. Discover what many different insects do in winter in this picture book.

Herriges, Ann. *Fall.* Minneapolis: Bellwether Media, 2007. Learn more about what happens during fall, a season filled with changes.

WEBSITES

Black Bears
http://www.state.nj.us/dep/fgw/bearfacts_kids.htm
Play games and discover what to do if you see a black bear.

Migrating Animal Printouts
http://www.zoomschool.com/coloring/migrate.shtml
Learn about different animals from around the world that migrate.

Monarch Watch
http://www.monarchwatch.org/
Help track the migration of monarch butterflies.

INDEX